Life Cycles

Frogs and Toads

Julie K. Lundgren

www.rourkepublishing.com

www.rourkepublishing.com

Photo credits: Cover © Wolfgang Staib, Dr. Morley Read, Pletnyakov Peter, Michael D. Barnes; Title Page © Michael D. Barnes; Contents © Eduard Kyslynskyy, Splash, Daniel Petrescu; Page 4 © David Anderson; Page 5 © Denis Tabler; Page 6 © Eduard Kyslynskyy, Eric Isselée, David Anderson; Page 7 © FloridaStock; Page 8 © hug(o)photo; Page 9 © Splash; Page 10 © worldswildlifewonders; Page 11 © Dawid Legwant, Christian Fischer; Page 12 © Payless Images; Page 13 © dabjola, Jason Mintzer; Page 14 © hagit berkovich; Page 15 © Art_man; Page 16 © Darren J. Bradley; Page 17 © worldswildlifewonders; Page 19 © Dr. Morley Read, Chris Alcock, davidundderriese, Jason Mintzer; Page 20 © Daniel Petrescu; Page 22 © Splash, dabjola, Dr. Morley Read, hagit berkovich

Editor: Jeanne Sturm

Cover and page design by Nicola Stratford, bdpublishing.com

Library of Congress Cataloging-in-Publication Data

Lundgren, Julie K.
  Frogs and toads / Julie K. Lundgren.
    p. cm. -- (Life cycles)
Includes bibliographical references and index.
ISBN 978-1-61590-309-2 ((Hard Cover) alk. paper)
ISBN 978-1-61590-548-5 (Soft Cover)
1. Frogs--Juvenile literature. 2. Toads--Juvenile literature. I. Title.
QL668.E2L86 2011
597.8'9--dc22
                    2010009026

Rourke Publishing
Printed in the United States of America, North Mankato, Minnesota
033010
033010LP

www.rourkepublishing.com - rourke@rourkepublishing.com
Post Office Box 643328, Vero Beach, Florida 32964

Table of Contents

Leapers and Peepers

What animals first live under water and later can live on land and breathe air? Frogs and toads! These **amphibians** have special, changing bodies that let them live on land and in the water at different times in their lives.

Amphibians are **ectotherms**. They raise and lower their body temperature using the air or water around them. They do not make their own heat like people.

American toads warm up in the Sun. To cool down, they get wet or sit in the shade.

4

Spring peepers get their name from the sound they make.

The smallest frog can fit on the tip of your nose. The largest fills a dinner plate!

Frogs make big leaps using their long, strong legs.

Generally, frogs have smooth skin, slender bodies, and long back legs. Many toads have bumpy skin and short, squat bodies. However, they both pass air and water through their skin and need moist homes. Frogs and toads are more alike than different.

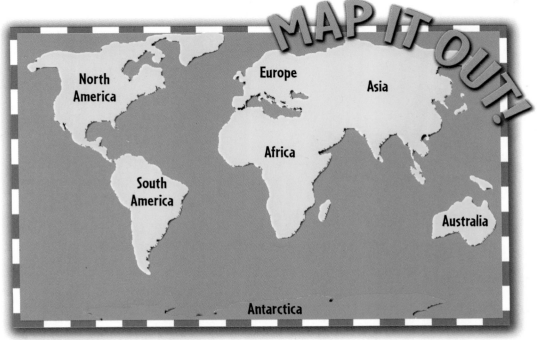

North America

Europe

Asia

Africa

South America

Australia

Antarctica

The world's more than 4,000 kinds of frogs and toads live on every continent but Antarctica. The greatest numbers live in tropical rainforests.

Many animals eat frogs and toads. They give people an idea about habitat health, too. Frogs and toads cannot live in **polluted** places.

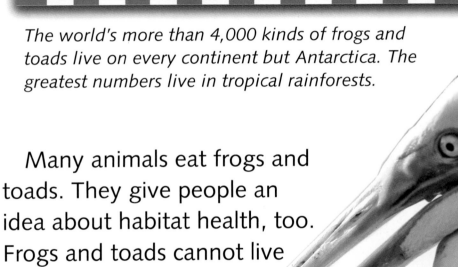

Small Start

In different ways, Earth's living things start, grow, **reproduce**, and die. As frogs and toads go through their **life cycle**, their bodies change shape. They start life as small, soft eggs.

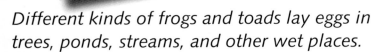

Different kinds of frogs and toads lay eggs in trees, ponds, streams, and other wet places.

DID YOU KNOW?

Amphibians lay eggs without shells. The eggs look like little sacs of liquid surrounded by protective jelly.

Many frogs and toads lay eggs and leave. Others care for their eggs. They may carry the eggs with them or guard them.

Glass frogs guard their eggs.

DID YOU KNOW?

The male midwife toad carries his mate's eggs on his back until they hatch.

A Tadpole's World

After about a week, tadpoles hatch from the eggs. Like fish, tadpoles have tails for swimming and **gills** for breathing. Their eyes look out from the sides of their heads. Young tadpoles have no legs.

Cycle Snapshot

Tadpoles eat **algae** and other tiny plants.

Tree frogs may lay their eggs on a leaf overhanging a pond.
As the eggs hatch, the tadpoles plop into the water.

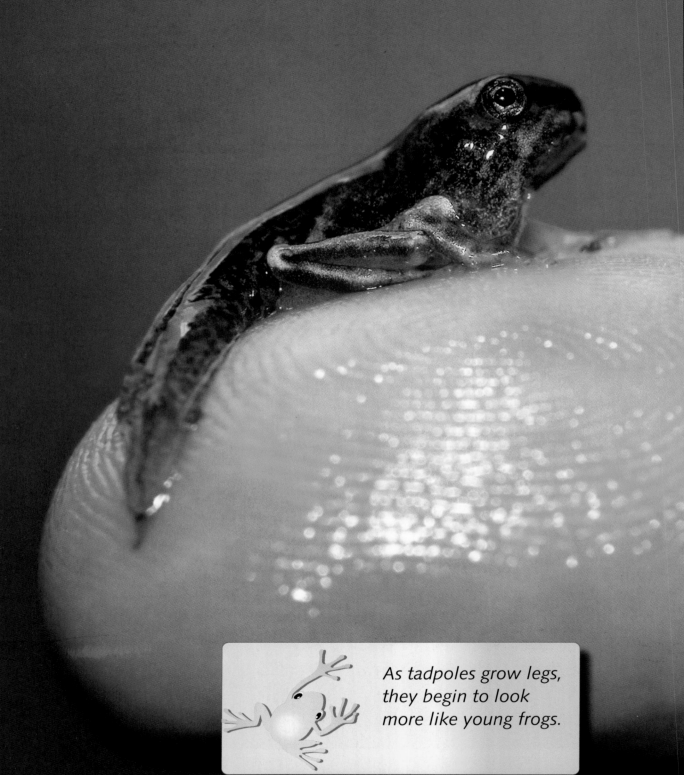

As tadpoles grow legs, they begin to look more like young frogs.

Frogs and toads may lay many eggs at once, in the hope that at least a few will survive. A few kinds of frogs and toads carry their tadpoles to protect them.

Tadpoles grow legs and lungs. Their tails shrink and their eyes move to face forward. Their bodies get ready to live out of the water.

DID YOU KNOW?

Tadpoles, and frogs, have teeth.

The tadpoles of North America's largest frog, the American bullfrog, take two to three years to change into frogs.

The tadpole stage usually lasts one to three weeks. Some kinds, though, spend the winter as tadpoles and change into adults in the spring. For American bullfrogs, the extra time and growth as tadpoles makes for larger adults.

DID YOU KNOW?

Strawberry poison dart frog mothers lay an egg daily for each tadpole to eat.

Hopping Hunters

As adults, frogs and toads learn how to live in yet another new world. Most now eat only other animals, like insects and worms. They have new enemies like birds, snakes, and raccoons. They must learn to hunt and avoid other hunters.

Color forms a defense. Poisonous frogs and toads use their bold colors to warn away hungry animals. Green or brown frogs and toads remain unseen.

White's tree frog can change from brown to green and back again.

As it finishes transforming into an adult, a young frog's tail will continue to shrink.

Deadly poison dart frogs come in a rainbow of bright colors.

The common spadefoot toad spends the winter deep in the soil.

In cold areas, toads survive winter by **hibernating**. Some dig down to where frost cannot reach. Wood frogs make **antifreeze** for their bodies. They freeze, but thaw in the spring unharmed.

In deserts, frogs and toads stay deep in the ground until heavy rains awaken them. This may only happen once a year.

HELP THOSE HOPPERS!

Busy roads, habitat loss, **climate change**, and pollution endanger amphibians. Help them by keeping the Earth clean. Do not keep wild frogs or toads as pets. Look, listen, and learn, and then let them be.

Life Cycle Round-up

1 Frogs and toads begin as eggs.

4 Adults find mates and begin the cycle again.

2 Tadpoles hatch from eggs.

3 Tadpoles eat, grow, and change into adults.

Glossary

algae (AL-jee): tiny, green, floating plants that grow in water

amphibians (am-FIB-ee-uhnz): certain animals, including frogs and toads, that first use gills and then use lungs to breathe

antifreeze (AN-tee-freez): a chemical some frogs make in their bodies to keep them safe during hibernation

climate change (KLYE-mit CHAYNJ): changes in the Earth's weather that affect animal habitats

ectotherms (ECK-toe-thermz): animals who control their body temperature by using their environment

gills (GILZ): special body parts of fish and amphibians that help them breathe underwater

hibernating (HYE-bur-nay-ting): greatly slowing down the body's systems in order to survive poor or cold conditions

life cycle (LIFE SY-kuhl): the process of all life on Earth where a living thing begins, grows, reproduces, and then dies

polluted (puh-LOO-tehd): unhealthy, not clean, or containing harmful poisons

reproduce (ree-pruh-DOOSS): make more of something

Index

Websites to Visit

www.allaboutfrogs.org/

www.pbs.org/wnet/nature/episodes/frogs-the-thin-green-line/
   introduction/4763/

www.environment.nsw.gov.au/buddies/BackyardBuddiesFrogs.htm

www.animaldiversity.ummz.umich.edu/site/topics/frogCalls.html

www.dnr.wi.gov/eek/

www.biokids.umich.edu/critters/Anura/

About the Author

Julie K. Lundgren grew up near Lake Superior where she reveled in mucking about in the woods, picking berries, and expanding her rock collection. Her appetite for learning about nature led her to a degree in biology from the University of Minnesota. She currently lives in Minnesota with her husband and two sons.

24